AB

Name	Name
Address	Address
Telephone	Telephone
Email	Email
Name	Name
Address	Address
Telephone	Telephone
Email	Email
Name	Name
Address	Address
Telephone	Telephone
Email	Email

Name	Name
Address	Address
Telephone	Telephone
Email	Email

Name	Name
Address	Address
Telephone	Telephone
Email	Email

Name	Name
Address	Address
Telephone	Telephone
Email	Email

AB

Name	Name
Address	Address
Telephone	Telephone
Email	Email
Name	Name
Address	Address
Telephone	Telephone
Email	Email
Name	Name
Address	Address
Telephone	Telephone
Email	Email

Name
Address

Telephone
Email

Name
Address

Telephone
Email

Name
Address

Telephone
Email

Name
Address

Telephone
Email

Name
Address

Telephone
Email

Name
Address

Telephone
Email

AB

| Name | Name |
| Address | Address |

Telephone
Email

Telephone
Email

Name
Address

Name
Address

Telephone
Email

Telephone
Email

Name
Address

Name
Address

Telephone
Email

Telephone
Email

Name	Name
Address	Address
Telephone	Telephone
Email	Email

Name	Name
Address	Address
Telephone	Telephone
Email	Email

Name	Name
Address	Address
Telephone	Telephone
Email	Email

AB

Name	Name
Address	Address
Telephone	Telephone
Email	Email

Name	Name
Address	Address
Telephone	Telephone
Email	Email

Name	Name
Address	Address
Telephone	Telephone
Email	Email

Name	Name
Address	Address
Telephone	Telephone
Email	Email

Name	Name
Address	Address
Telephone	Telephone
Email	Email

Name	Name
Address	Address
Telephone	Telephone
Email	Email

AB

Name	Name
Address	Address
Telephone	Telephone
Email	Email

Name	Name
Address	Address
Telephone	Telephone
Email	Email

Name	Name
Address	Address
Telephone	Telephone
Email	Email

Name	Name
Address	Address
Telephone	Telephone
Email	Email

Name	Name
Address	Address
Telephone	Telephone
Email	Email

Name	Name
Address	Address
Telephone	Telephone
Email	Email

CD

| Name | Name |
| Address | Address |

Telephone
Email

Name
Address

Telephone
Email

Name
Address

Telephone
Email

Name
Address

Telephone
Email

Name
Address

Telephone
Email

Name
Address

Telephone
Email

Name	Name
Address	Address
Telephone	Telephone
Email	Email

Name	Name
Address	Address
Telephone	Telephone
Email	Email

Name	Name
Address	Address
Telephone	Telephone
Email	Email

CD

| Name | Name |
| Address | Address |

Telephone | Telephone
Email | Email

Name | Name
Address | Address

Telephone | Telephone
Email | Email

Name | Name
Address | Address

Telephone | Telephone
Email | Email

Name	Name
Address	Address
Telephone	Telephone
Email	Email

Name	Name
Address	Address
Telephone	Telephone
Email	Email

Name	Name
Address	Address
Telephone	Telephone
Email	Email

CD

Name	Name
Address	Address
Telephone	Telephone
Email	Email

Name	Name
Address	Address
Telephone	Telephone
Email	Email

Name	Name
Address	Address
Telephone	Telephone
Email	Email

Name	Name
Address	Address
Telephone	Telephone
Email	Email

Name	Name
Address	Address
Telephone	Telephone
Email	Email

Name	Name
Address	Address
Telephone	Telephone
Email	Email

CD

Name
Address

Telephone
Email

Name
Address

Telephone
Email

Name
Address

Telephone
Email

Name
Address

Telephone
Email

Name
Address

Telephone
Email

Name
Address

Telephone
Email

| Name | Name |
| Address | Address |

Telephone | Telephone
Email | Email

Name | Name
Address | Address

Telephone | Telephone
Email | Email

Name | Name
Address | Address

Telephone | Telephone
Email | Email

CD

Name
Address

Telephone
Email

Name
Address

Telephone
Email

Name
Address

Telephone
Email

Name
Address

Telephone
Email

Name
Address

Telephone
Email

Name
Address

Telephone
Email

Name	Name
Address	Address
Telephone	Telephone
Email	Email
Name	Name
Address	Address
Telephone	Telephone
Email	Email
Name	Name
Address	Address
Telephone	Telephone
Email	Email

Name
Address

Telephone
Email

Name
Address

Telephone
Email

Name
Address

Telephone
Email

Name
Address

Telephone
Email

Name
Address

Telephone
Email

Name
Address

Telephone
Email

EF

Name ....
Address ....
....
....
Telephone ....
Email ....

Name ....
Address ....
....
....
Telephone ....
Email ....

Name ....
Address ....
....
....
Telephone ....
Email ....

Name ....
Address ....
....
....
Telephone ....
Email ....

Name ....
Address ....
....
....
Telephone ....
Email ....

Name ....
Address ....
....
....
Telephone ....
Email ....

Name	Name
Address	Address
Telephone	Telephone
Email	Email

Name	Name
Address	Address
Telephone	Telephone
Email	Email

Name	Name
Address	Address
Telephone	Telephone
Email	Email

EF

Name	Name
Address	Address
Telephone	Telephone
Email	Email
Name	Name
Address	Address
Telephone	Telephone
Email	Email
Name	Name
Address	Address
Telephone	Telephone
Email	Email

EF

Name
Address

Telephone
Email

Name
Address

Telephone
Email

Name
Address

Telephone
Email

Name
Address

Telephone
Email

Name
Address

Telephone
Email

Name
Address

Telephone
Email

Name
Address

Telephone
Email

Name
Address

Telephone
Email

Name
Address

Telephone
Email

Name
Address

Telephone
Email

Name
Address

Telephone
Email

Name
Address

Telephone
Email

EF

Name	Name
Address	Address
Telephone	Telephone
Email	Email
Name	Name
Address	Address
Telephone	Telephone
Email	Email
Name	Name
Address	Address
Telephone	Telephone
Email	Email

Name
Address

Telephone
Email

Name
Address

Telephone
Email

Name
Address

Telephone
Email

Name
Address

Telephone
Email

Name
Address

Telephone
Email

Name
Address

Telephone
Email

Name	Name
Address	Address
Telephone	Telephone
Email	Email

Name	Name
Address	Address
Telephone	Telephone
Email	Email

Name	Name
Address	Address
Telephone	Telephone
Email	Email

EF

Name	Name
Address	Address
Telephone	Telephone
Email	Email

Name	Name
Address	Address
Telephone	Telephone
Email	Email

Name	Name
Address	Address
Telephone	Telephone
Email	Email

Name	Name
Address	Address
Telephone	Telephone
Email	Email

Name	Name
Address	Address
Telephone	Telephone
Email	Email

Name	Name
Address	Address
Telephone	Telephone
Email	Email

GH

Name	Name
Address	Address
Telephone	Telephone
Email	Email

Name	Name
Address	Address
Telephone	Telephone
Email	Email

Name	Name
Address	Address
Telephone	Telephone
Email	Email

Name	Name
Address	Address
Telephone	Telephone
Email	Email

Name	Name
Address	Address
Telephone	Telephone
Email	Email

Name	Name
Address	Address
Telephone	Telephone
Email	Email

GH

Name	Name
Address	Address
Telephone	Telephone
Email	Email

Name	Name
Address	Address
Telephone	Telephone
Email	Email

Name	Name
Address	Address
Telephone	Telephone
Email	Email

GH

Name
Address

Telephone
Email

Name
Address

Telephone
Email

Name
Address

Telephone
Email

Name
Address

Telephone
Email

Name
Address

Telephone
Email

Name
Address

Telephone
Email

Name
Address

Telephone
Email

Name
Address

Telephone
Email

Name
Address

Telephone
Email

Name
Address

Telephone
Email

Name
Address

Telephone
Email

Name
Address

Telephone
Email

GH

Name	Name
Address	Address
Telephone	Telephone
Email	Email

Name	Name
Address	Address
Telephone	Telephone
Email	Email

Name	Name
Address	Address
Telephone	Telephone
Email	Email

Name	Name
Address	Address
Telephone	Telephone
Email	Email

Name	Name
Address	Address
Telephone	Telephone
Email	Email

Name	Name
Address	Address
Telephone	Telephone
Email	Email

Name
Address

Telephone
Email

Name
Address

Telephone
Email

Name
Address

Telephone
Email

Name
Address

Telephone
Email

Name
Address

Telephone
Email

Name
Address

Telephone
Email

GH

Name	Name
Address	Address
Telephone	Telephone
Email	Email

Name	Name
Address	Address
Telephone	Telephone
Email	Email

Name	Name
Address	Address
Telephone	Telephone
Email	Email

Name
Address

Telephone
Email

Name
Address

Telephone
Email

Name
Address

Telephone
Email

Name
Address

Telephone
Email

Name
Address

Telephone
Email

Name
Address

Telephone
Email

Name	Name
Address	Address
Telephone	Telephone
Email	Email
Name	Name
Address	Address
Telephone	Telephone
Email	Email
Name	Name
Address	Address
Telephone	Telephone
Email	Email

Name	Name
Address	Address
Telephone	Telephone
Email	Email

Name	Name
Address	Address
Telephone	Telephone
Email	Email

Name	Name
Address	Address
Telephone	Telephone
Email	Email

IJ

Name	Name
Address	Address
Telephone	Telephone
Email	Email

Name	Name
Address	Address
Telephone	Telephone
Email	Email

Name	Name
Address	Address
Telephone	Telephone
Email	Email

Name	Name
Address	Address
Telephone	Telephone
Email	Email

Name	Name
Address	Address
Telephone	Telephone
Email	Email

Name	Name
Address	Address
Telephone	Telephone
Email	Email

Name
Address

Telephone
Email

Name
Address

Telephone
Email

Name
Address

Telephone
Email

Name
Address

Telephone
Email

Name
Address

Telephone
Email

Name
Address

Telephone
Email

Name
Address

Telephone
Email

Name
Address

Telephone
Email

Name
Address

Telephone
Email

Name
Address

Telephone
Email

Name
Address

Telephone
Email

Name
Address

Telephone
Email

Name	Name
Address	Address
Telephone	Telephone
Email	Email

Name	Name
Address	Address
Telephone	Telephone
Email	Email

Name	Name
Address	Address
Telephone	Telephone
Email	Email

Name	Name
Address	Address
Telephone	Telephone
Email	Email
Name	Name
Address	Address
Telephone	Telephone
Email	Email
Name	Name
Address	Address
Telephone	Telephone
Email	Email

Name
Address

Telephone
Email

Name
Address

Telephone
Email

Name
Address

Telephone
Email

Name
Address

Telephone
Email

Name
Address

Telephone
Email

Name
Address

Telephone
Email

Name	Name
Address	Address
Telephone	Telephone
Email	Email
Name	Name
Address	Address
Telephone	Telephone
Email	Email
Name	Name
Address	Address
Telephone	Telephone
Email	Email

Name
Address

Telephone
Email

Name
Address

Telephone
Email

Name
Address

Telephone
Email

Name
Address

Telephone
Email

Name
Address

Telephone
Email

Name
Address

Telephone
Email

Name	Name
Address	Address
Telephone	Telephone
Email	Email

Name	Name
Address	Address
Telephone	Telephone
Email	Email

Name	Name
Address	Address
Telephone	Telephone
Email	Email

KL

Name
Address

Telephone
Email

Name
Address

Telephone
Email

Name
Address

Telephone
Email

Name
Address

Telephone
Email

Name
Address

Telephone
Email

Name
Address

Telephone
Email

Name	Name
Address	Address
Telephone	Telephone
Email	Email

Name	Name
Address	Address
Telephone	Telephone
Email	Email

Name	Name
Address	Address
Telephone	Telephone
Email	Email

KL

Name
Address

Telephone
Email

Name
Address

Telephone
Email

Name
Address

Telephone
Email

Name
Address

Telephone
Email

Name
Address

Telephone
Email

Name
Address

Telephone
Email

Name	Name
Address	Address
Telephone	Telephone
Email	Email

Name	Name
Address	Address
Telephone	Telephone
Email	Email

Name	Name
Address	Address
Telephone	Telephone
Email	Email

KL

Name
Address

Telephone
Email

Name
Address

Telephone
Email

Name
Address

Telephone
Email

Name
Address

Telephone
Email

Name
Address

Telephone
Email

Name
Address

Telephone
Email

Name	Name
Address	Address
Telephone	Telephone
Email	Email
Name	Name
Address	Address
Telephone	Telephone
Email	Email
Name	Name
Address	Address
Telephone	Telephone
Email	Email

KL

Name
Address

Telephone
Email

Name
Address

Telephone
Email

Name
Address

Telephone
Email

Name
Address

Telephone
Email

Name
Address

Telephone
Email

Name
Address

Telephone
Email

Name
Address

Telephone
Email

Name
Address

Telephone
Email

Name
Address

Telephone
Email

Name
Address

Telephone
Email

Name
Address

Telephone
Email

Name
Address

Telephone
Email

MN

Name	Name
Address	Address
Telephone	Telephone
Email	Email

Name	Name
Address	Address
Telephone	Telephone
Email	Email

Name	Name
Address	Address
Telephone	Telephone
Email	Email

Name	Name
Address	Address
Telephone	Telephone
Email	Email

Name	Name
Address	Address
Telephone	Telephone
Email	Email

Name	Name
Address	Address
Telephone	Telephone
Email	Email

MN

Name	Name
Address	Address
Telephone	Telephone
Email	Email
Name	Name
Address	Address
Telephone	Telephone
Email	Email
Name	Name
Address	Address
Telephone	Telephone
Email	Email

Name	Name
Address	Address
Telephone	Telephone
Email	Email
Name	Name
Address	Address
Telephone	Telephone
Email	Email
Name	Name
Address	Address
Telephone	Telephone
Email	Email

MN

Name	Name
Address	Address
Telephone	Telephone
Email	Email

Name	Name
Address	Address
Telephone	Telephone
Email	Email

Name	Name
Address	Address
Telephone	Telephone
Email	Email

Name Address Telephone Email	Name Address Telephone Email
Name Address Telephone Email	Name Address Telephone Email
Name Address Telephone Email	Name Address Telephone Email

MN

Name
Address

Telephone
Email

Name
Address

Telephone
Email

Name
Address

Telephone
Email

Name
Address

Telephone
Email

Name
Address

Telephone
Email

Name
Address

Telephone
Email

Name
Address

Telephone
Email

Name
Address

Telephone
Email

Name
Address

Telephone
Email

Name
Address

Telephone
Email

Name
Address

Telephone
Email

Name
Address

Telephone
Email

MN

Name	Name
Address	Address
Telephone	Telephone
Email	Email

Name	Name
Address	Address
Telephone	Telephone
Email	Email

Name	Name
Address	Address
Telephone	Telephone
Email	Email

Name	Name
Address	Address
Telephone	Telephone
Email	Email

Name	Name
Address	Address
Telephone	Telephone
Email	Email

Name	Name
Address	Address
Telephone	Telephone
Email	Email

Name	Name
Address	Address
Telephone	Telephone
Email	Email

Name	Name
Address	Address
Telephone	Telephone
Email	Email

Name	Name
Address	Address
Telephone	Telephone
Email	Email

Name	Name
Address	Address
Telephone	Telephone
Email	Email
Name	Name
Address	Address
Telephone	Telephone
Email	Email
Name	Name
Address	Address
Telephone	Telephone
Email	Email

OP

Name
Address

Telephone
Email

Name
Address

Telephone
Email

Name
Address

Telephone
Email

Name
Address

Telephone
Email

Name
Address

Telephone
Email

Name
Address

Telephone
Email

Name	Name
Address	Address
Telephone	Telephone
Email	Email

Name	Name
Address	Address
Telephone	Telephone
Email	Email

Name	Name
Address	Address
Telephone	Telephone
Email	Email

| Name | Name |
| Address | Address |

Telephone | Telephone
Email | Email

Name | Name
Address | Address

Telephone | Telephone
Email | Email

Name | Name
Address | Address

Telephone | Telephone
Email | Email

Name	Name
Address	Address
Telephone	Telephone
Email	Email

Name	Name
Address	Address
Telephone	Telephone
Email	Email

Name	Name
Address	Address
Telephone	Telephone
Email	Email

Name
Address

Telephone
Email

Name
Address

Telephone
Email

Name
Address

Telephone
Email

Name
Address

Telephone
Email

Name
Address

Telephone
Email

Name
Address

Telephone
Email

Name	Name
Address	Address
Telephone	Telephone
Email	Email

Name	Name
Address	Address
Telephone	Telephone
Email	Email

Name	Name
Address	Address
Telephone	Telephone
Email	Email

OP

Name
Address

Telephone
Email

Name
Address

Telephone
Email

Name
Address

Telephone
Email

Name
Address

Telephone
Email

Name
Address

Telephone
Email

Name
Address

Telephone
Email

Name	Name
Address	Address
Telephone	Telephone
Email	Email

Name	Name
Address	Address
Telephone	Telephone
Email	Email

Name	Name
Address	Address
Telephone	Telephone
Email	Email

Name	Name
Address	Address
Telephone	Telephone
Email	Email

Name	Name
Address	Address
Telephone	Telephone
Email	Email

Name	Name
Address	Address
Telephone	Telephone
Email	Email

Name	Name
Address	Address
Telephone	Telephone
Email	Email

Name	Name
Address	Address
Telephone	Telephone
Email	Email

Name	Name
Address	Address
Telephone	Telephone
Email	Email

Name
Address

Telephone
Email

Name
Address

Telephone
Email

Name
Address

Telephone
Email

Name
Address

Telephone
Email

Name
Address

Telephone
Email

Name
Address

Telephone
Email

Name	Name
Address	Address
Telephone	Telephone
Email	Email

Name	Name
Address	Address
Telephone	Telephone
Email	Email

Name	Name
Address	Address
Telephone	Telephone
Email	Email

QR

Name	Name
Address	Address
Telephone	Telephone
Email	Email
Name	Name
Address	Address
Telephone	Telephone
Email	Email
Name	Name
Address	Address
Telephone	Telephone
Email	Email

Name	Name
Address	Address
Telephone	Telephone
Email	Email

Name	Name
Address	Address
Telephone	Telephone
Email	Email

Name	Name
Address	Address
Telephone	Telephone
Email	Email

Name	Name
Address	Address
Telephone	Telephone
Email	Email

Name	Name
Address	Address
Telephone	Telephone
Email	Email

Name	Name
Address	Address
Telephone	Telephone
Email	Email

Name	Name
Address	Address
Telephone	Telephone
Email	Email

Name	Name
Address	Address
Telephone	Telephone
Email	Email

Name	Name
Address	Address
Telephone	Telephone
Email	Email

QR

Name
Address

Telephone
Email

Name
Address

Telephone
Email

Name
Address

Telephone
Email

Name
Address

Telephone
Email

Name
Address

Telephone
Email

Name
Address

Telephone
Email

Name	Name
Address	Address
Telephone	Telephone
Email	Email

Name	Name
Address	Address
Telephone	Telephone
Email	Email

Name	Name
Address	Address
Telephone	Telephone
Email	Email

ST

Name	Name
Address	Address
Telephone	Telephone
Email	Email

Name	Name
Address	Address
Telephone	Telephone
Email	Email

Name	Name
Address	Address
Telephone	Telephone
Email	Email

Name	Name
Address	Address
Telephone	Telephone
Email	Email
Name	Name
Address	Address
Telephone	Telephone
Email	Email
Name	Name
Address	Address
Telephone	Telephone
Email	Email

ST

Name	Name
Address	Address
Telephone	Telephone
Email	Email

Name	Name
Address	Address
Telephone	Telephone
Email	Email

Name	Name
Address	Address
Telephone	Telephone
Email	Email

Name	Name
Address	Address
Telephone	Telephone
Email	Email

Name	Name
Address	Address
Telephone	Telephone
Email	Email

Name	Name
Address	Address
Telephone	Telephone
Email	Email

ST

Name	Name
Address	Address
Telephone	Telephone
Email	Email

Name	Name
Address	Address
Telephone	Telephone
Email	Email

Name	Name
Address	Address
Telephone	Telephone
Email	Email

Name	Name
Address	Address
Telephone	Telephone
Email	Email

Name	Name
Address	Address
Telephone	Telephone
Email	Email

Name	Name
Address	Address
Telephone	Telephone
Email	Email

ST

Name
Address

Telephone
Email

Name
Address

Telephone
Email

Name
Address

Telephone
Email

Name
Address

Telephone
Email

Name
Address

Telephone
Email

Name
Address

Telephone
Email

Name
Address

Telephone
Email

Name
Address

Telephone
Email

Name
Address

Telephone
Email

Name
Address

Telephone
Email

Name
Address

Telephone
Email

Name
Address

Telephone
Email

ST

Name
Address

Telephone
Email

Name
Address

Telephone
Email

Name
Address

Telephone
Email

Name
Address

Telephone
Email

Name
Address

Telephone
Email

Name
Address

Telephone
Email

Name	Name
Address	Address
Telephone	Telephone
Email	Email
Name	Name
Address	Address
Telephone	Telephone
Email	Email
Name	Name
Address	Address
Telephone	Telephone
Email	Email

UV

Name	Name
Address	Address
Telephone	Telephone
Email	Email

Name	Name
Address	Address
Telephone	Telephone
Email	Email

Name	Name
Address	Address
Telephone	Telephone
Email	Email

Name	Name
Address	Address
Telephone	Telephone
Email	Email
Name	Name
Address	Address
Telephone	Telephone
Email	Email
Name	Name
Address	Address
Telephone	Telephone
Email	Email

UV

Name	Name
Address	Address
Telephone	Telephone
Email	Email
Name	Name
Address	Address
Telephone	Telephone
Email	Email
Name	Name
Address	Address
Telephone	Telephone
Email	Email

Name
Address

Telephone
Email

Name
Address

Telephone
Email

Name
Address

Telephone
Email

Name
Address

Telephone
Email

Name
Address

Telephone
Email

Name
Address

Telephone
Email

UV

Name	Name
Address	Address
Telephone	Telephone
Email	Email

Name	Name
Address	Address
Telephone	Telephone
Email	Email

Name	Name
Address	Address
Telephone	Telephone
Email	Email

Name	Name
Address	Address
Telephone	Telephone
Email	Email
Name	Name
Address	Address
Telephone	Telephone
Email	Email
Name	Name
Address	Address
Telephone	Telephone
Email	Email

UV

Name
Address

Telephone
Email

Name
Address

Telephone
Email

Name
Address

Telephone
Email

Name
Address

Telephone
Email

Name
Address

Telephone
Email

Name
Address

Telephone
Email

Name	Name
Address	Address
Telephone	Telephone
Email	Email
Name	Name
Address	Address
Telephone	Telephone
Email	Email
Name	Name
Address	Address
Telephone	Telephone
Email	Email

UV

Name	Name
Address	Address
Telephone	Telephone
Email	Email

Name	Name
Address	Address
Telephone	Telephone
Email	Email

Name	Name
Address	Address
Telephone	Telephone
Email	Email

Name
Address

Telephone
Email

Name
Address

Telephone
Email

Name
Address

Telephone
Email

Name
Address

Telephone
Email

Name
Address

Telephone
Email

Name
Address

Telephone
Email

WX

Name	Name
Address	Address
Telephone	Telephone
Email	Email

Name	Name
Address	Address
Telephone	Telephone
Email	Email

Name	Name
Address	Address
Telephone	Telephone
Email	Email

Name
Address

Telephone
Email

Name
Address

Telephone
Email

Name
Address

Telephone
Email

Name
Address

Telephone
Email

Name
Address

Telephone
Email

Name
Address

Telephone
Email

Name
Address

Telephone
Email

Name
Address

Telephone
Email

Name
Address

Telephone
Email

Name
Address

Telephone
Email

Name
Address

Telephone
Email

Name
Address

Telephone
Email

Name
Address

Telephone
Email

Name
Address

Telephone
Email

Name
Address

Telephone
Email

Name
Address

Telephone
Email

Name
Address

Telephone
Email

Name
Address

Telephone
Email

Name	Name
Address	Address
Telephone	Telephone
Email	Email

Name	Name
Address	Address
Telephone	Telephone
Email	Email

Name	Name
Address	Address
Telephone	Telephone
Email	Email

Name	Name
Address	Address
Telephone	Telephone
Email	Email
Name	Name
Address	Address
Telephone	Telephone
Email	Email
Name	Name
Address	Address
Telephone	Telephone
Email	Email

Name
Address

Telephone
Email

Name
Address

Telephone
Email

Name
Address

Telephone
Email

Name
Address

Telephone
Email

Name
Address

Telephone
Email

Name
Address

Telephone
Email

Name	Name
Address	Address
Telephone	Telephone
Email	Email

Name	Name
Address	Address
Telephone	Telephone
Email	Email

Name	Name
Address	Address
Telephone	Telephone
Email	Email

Name
Address

Telephone
Email

Name
Address

Telephone
Email

Name
Address

Telephone
Email

Name
Address

Telephone
Email

Name
Address

Telephone
Email

Name
Address

Telephone
Email

Name	Name
Address	Address
Telephone	Telephone
Email	Email
Name	Name
Address	Address
Telephone	Telephone
Email	Email
Name	Name
Address	Address
Telephone	Telephone
Email	Email

Name	Name ....
Address	Address ....
....	....
....	....
Telephone	Telephone ....
Email	Email ....
Name	Name ....
Address	Address ....
....	....
....	....
Telephone	Telephone ....
Email	Email ....
Name	Name ....
Address	Address ....
....	....
....	....
Telephone	Telephone ....
Email	Email ....

Name
Address

Telephone
Email

Name
Address

Telephone
Email

Name
Address

Telephone
Email

Name
Address

Telephone
Email

Name
Address

Telephone
Email

Name
Address

Telephone
Email

Name
Address

Telephone
Email

Name
Address

Telephone
Email

Name
Address

Telephone
Email

Name
Address

Telephone
Email

Name
Address

Telephone
Email

Name
Address

Telephone
Email

Name	Name
Address	Address
Telephone	Telephone
Email	Email

Name	Name
Address	Address
Telephone	Telephone
Email	Email

Name	Name
Address	Address
Telephone	Telephone
Email	Email

YZ

Name ....
Address ....
....

Telephone ....
Email ....

Name ....
Address ....
....

Telephone ....
Email ....

Name ....
Address ....
....

Telephone ....
Email ....

Name ....
Address ....
....

Telephone ....
Email ....

Name ....
Address ....
....

Telephone ....
Email ....

Name ....
Address ....
....

Telephone ....
Email ....

Name
Address

Telephone
Email

Name
Address

Telephone
Email

Name
Address

Telephone
Email

Name
Address

Telephone
Email

Name
Address

Telephone
Email

Name
Address

Telephone
Email

Name	Name
Address	Address
Telephone	Telephone
Email	Email

Name	Name
Address	Address
Telephone	Telephone
Email	Email

Name	Name
Address	Address
Telephone	Telephone
Email	Email